I0191163

ABCs of Classroom Management

Cheryl Ann Busby

Copyright © 2014 Cheryl Ann Busby

All rights reserved.

ISBN: 0692102221
ISBN-13: 978-0692102220

DEDICATION

To my family: Ricky, Elizabeth, Sarah, Nanna,
grandparents, uncles, aunts, sisters, brothers, and cousins
To educators and students everywhere

CONTENTS

ACKNOWLEDGMENTS

In an effort to provide on time motivation for teachers
everywhere, this mini book was developed from
experiences of 20+ years in public education.

1 A..B..C..D..

A: Acknowledge All

According to Merriam-Webster, when you acknowledge someone, you provide a positive recognition. Greeting your students will help create an environment of respect. When you acknowledge and greet your students, you are saying, "You are important to me and to your classmates." When students know that they are valued, they are motivated to value teachers, other students, rules, etc...This simple acknowledgement and welcome can brighten any student's day and set them on a path of success

B: Be Prepared!

Teachers must be prepared physically, emotionally, academically, and spiritually for the students that daily enter the classroom. Your emotions have a lot to do with your classroom environment. If you are calm, your students will be calm. Your students follow your lead. Practice thinking and speaking positive things about your students. A positive outlook will cause you to expect the best of all of your students. Spend time meditating on things that are good and of a good report in reference to your students, job, etc. Prepare lesson plans for every subject. Gather all your materials in advance. Everything should be ready for your students. Get some exercise. Walking, for example, will boost your spirits and give you energy for each day.

C: Communicate

During the first weeks of school, you must communicate your rules and procedures for classroom success. Do not assume that your students know what is expected of them. You must teach and model what is expected of them.

Teach and model: How to enter the Classroom; How to Make a Lunch Choice; How to and Where to Turn in Classwork; How to Ask for Help; How to Line Up; How to Walk in the Hall; How to Behave in the Bathroom; How to Act During Lunch; How to participate during Recess; How to come down to the Carpet for group time; What to do Next; How to Solve a Problem; How to Label Assignment Papers; How to Copy HW into an Agenda; etc.. For everything that you want your students to do, you must communicate how you want it done.

With your expectations, communicate your reward and consequence system. Students need to know that there are rewards for following rules and procedures. They also need to know that there are consequences when rules and procedures are not followed.

Communicate your Expectations with parents. Parents are there to help you and to help their child be successful. Work together for student success!

D: Discussions

Students like to talk. Provide opportunities for your students to talk and discuss: Topics of study; Misunderstandings of concepts; Concerns; Interests; etc. Create a community environment where your students feel that what they say is valued. Create an environment of higher order thinkers(Bloom's Taxonomy) through discussions. Allow students to ask questions, research answers, and share their findings.

E: Encourage Daily

Did you know that when you encourage students, you are inspiring them to have courage? Think about what your students need courage to do: Reading? Math? Science? or Geography? Provide encouragement for that task. Your positive encouragement will cause great exploits to be accomplished by your students. Your positive words will put your students in a place of tremendous success. So, encourage your students and build them up. Strengthen them with words of support and praise.

F: Fairness

Being fair to all students will create an atmosphere of trust, commitment, and respect. Showing partiality amongst students will create a negative learning environment. According to Merriam-Webster, being fair means that you do not show unfair bias in favor of something or someone. Everyone in your classroom should be treated fairly.

G: Grace

Provide grace to your students on a daily basis. Kindness, courtesy, and favor are synonyms for the word grace. Students will make mistakes. This is part of the learning process. Give your students many opportunities to be successful. When your students do make a mistake, remember to show grace towards them so that they are able to learn from their mistakes and move on. Your understanding ways will assist them in being successful in the future.

H: Happy

Be happy about what you do. Share your love for learning with your students. Synonyms for happy include: content, peaceful, satisfied, overjoyed, pleased, thrilled, glad, etc. If you are happy, then your students will not be discouraged, miserable, or depressed (antonyms for happy) about being in your classroom.

3 I..J..K..L..M..N..O

I: Interest

Based on your curricular standards, find topics that interest your students. When your students are interested in what they are learning, they will be engaged. If they are engaged, they will remain on task.

J: Jazz it up!

Don't bore your students. Jazz up their learning experience. Use technology daily to teach concepts. Provide opportunities for students to demonstrate their understanding using technology. You will be amazed at your students' engagement. When students are actively involved, off task behaviors are limited.

K: Know your students

Get to know your students through weekly discussions. Knowing your students will assist you in providing engaging learning activities that will meet their needs. When you truly know your students, it shows them that you care.

L: Listen, Listen, Listen

Listening is an art. Many times we hear students talk to us about various things, but are we truly "listening" to what they are saying? Listening requires concentration. When you truly listen to your students, you are able to determine the motive of their conversation, pinpoint the true problem of a situation, and recognize a cry for help. When you listen, you learn.

M: Model Expectations

What do you expect of your students? After you have voiced your expectations, Model it. Demonstrate how your expectations should look. How do you want your students to behave? Model it. How do you want your students to enter your classroom, make their lunch choice, turn in homework, turn in classwork, line up for lunch, walk in the hallway, participate in groups, and communicate with each other??? **MODEL IT!** You must teach or model what you expect your students to do. Model everything until you get the desired results!

N: Never raise your voice

A soft, calm voice can do wonders. Yelling should not be an option in the classroom. You are an adult who knows how to effectively communicate. When you model your expectations, you can communicate calmly to your students. Create an environment where your students respond to appropriate communication. When you talk to your students in a soft, calm voice, an atmosphere of safety, security, respect, and love is created.

O: Ownership of Learning

Students should take ownership of their learning. Provide an opportunity for students to set personal, academic goals. These goals should correspond to different benchmarks throughout the year. Students should set goals for reading, writing, math, etc.. Once they have set their goals for success, refer to the goals continually and allow students to track their own progress. Immediate feedback should be provided for all assessments or performance tasks. When students take ownership of their own learning, success will be inevitable!!

4 P..Q..R..S..T..U..V..W..X..Y.. Z

P: Problem Solving

Knowing how to solve problems is the key to student success. If your school provides a character education manual, use it daily. Provide mini-lessons on solving daily problems. If your school does not have a character education program, there are many resources that can be found in your local bookstore or on the internet. Your goal is to equip your students with the skills to make positive decisions in everyday life.

Q: Quickly redirect

Off task behavior should quickly be redirected in a calm and gentle manner. After you have taught and modeled your procedures and expected behaviors, it should be required that students adhere to them. When there are off task behaviors, redirect your students immediately to your expected behaviors. Teach your students to be positive models of excellent behavior. Praise excellent behavior often so that off task behavior is non-existent in your classroom.

R: Read

In order to keep students up to par academically and socially, reading is key. When you read to your students, you help increase their vocabulary, you demonstrate how fluent readers sound, and you also provide your students with the opportunity to comprehend text higher than their academic grade level. Reading to your students will increase their desire to read themselves. And when they read themselves, a whole new world is opened to them and for them!

S: Schedule

Students like to know what happens next. Post a daily schedule on your board or wall that lists the subjects/topics, activities, etc. and times at which they occur. When students know what happens next, it allows them to transition with ease.

T: Teamwork

Create a class environment of team effort. Students must be taught how to work together for a common goal or cause. Set expectations for your teams/groups. Provide multiple opportunities for students to work together in groups and pairs. Working as a team should provide an opportunity for all involved to shine. Assign each member a task. Everyone should feel great about their contribution to the assignment/task.

U: Understand

Understand your role as a teacher, instructor, counselor, administrator, etc. When you know who you are as an educator, you will be able to effectively carry out your assigned task. Knowing your position or calling will alleviate unnecessary frustrations.

V: V.I.P

Every student in your classroom should be on your V.I.P (Very important Person and Very Intelligent Person) list. Make it your goal to make every child feel valued and appreciated. Appreciate the gifts and talents that are represented in your classroom each day. Remember that each student who enters your classroom is intelligent in a variety of ways. Focus on the intelligence of every child. Remind your students that they are: smart, exceptional, skillful, brilliant, gifted, knowledgeable, and wise. Always focus on the positive aspects of your students. Your students will rise to your positive words and expectations!

W: Wait time

During class discussion, remember to provide adequate time for students to respond to your questions. Because students process information in different ways and at different times, waiting for them to respond demonstrates that what they say is important. Create an atmosphere where all students feel comfortable participating in classroom discussions.

X: Exams Differentiated

Differentiate your exams based on your student's academic needs. Exams can be paper/pencil, oral, portfolios, typed, projects, kinesthetic performances, on white boards, on computers, with GPS responders, etc. Do not create unnecessary stress for your students. Your goal is to determine what your students understand. Use a variety of methods to assess your students understanding of concepts taught.

Y: Yes, I can and I will!

This is the attitude that all educators and students should have!. Whatever challenge that's presented large or small, the students should voice out "I can and I will". This simple phrase is a great motivation for accomplishing a desired goal. Try it and experience the success it will create for you and your students.

Z: Zeal

Are your zealous about what you do? If not, you should be! Your zeal will be evident in your attitude, your words, and actions. Your zeal for math, reading, science, social studies, etc. will inspire a zeal for learning within your students. So, find your passion in education! Show your zeal! Allow others to reap the benefits of what you know!

May the suggestions in this book provide you and your students with timely words of encouragement and direction. You and your students deserve the best opportunity for success.

I would like to thank you personally for all that you do for students everywhere and on every level. Know that you are highly valued!

Value yourself! Value your students! Take care of yourself! Take care of your students!

Read and use this book every day!
Reflect on your day. Write it down!
Celebrate your success.
There's always something to celebrate.

Your Reflections:

ABOUT THE AUTHOR

Cheryl Busby

Educator
Bachelor of Science in Early Childhood Education
Master of Education in Curriculum and Instruction
Middle Grades Language Arts
Gifted Education

Cheryl resides in Fayette County, Georgia with husband, Ricky. Cheryl and Ricky have two grown daughters, Elizabeth and Sarah.

www.ingramcontent.com/pod-product-compliance
Lightning Source LLC
Chambersburg PA
CBHW070050040426
42331CB00034B/2988

* 9 7 8 0 6 9 2 1 0 2 2 2 0 *